美人魚上學趣

文／孟瑛如、陳惠珠
圖／張瓊瑤
英文翻譯／吳侑達

雖然我失去了聲音，但我可以到陸地上生活了。對我來說，一切都是新的開始……

今天要去上學了，我有一點開心，又有一點害怕，因為我從來沒有上過學！

　　突然有一隻小鳥飛過來，牠
停在樹枝上對著我說：

　　「美人魚！美人魚！妳不會
說話，又不會唱歌，怎麼敢去
上學啊？」

　　我聽了之後，便從書包拿出笛子，吹了一首「小星星」，小鳥聽了就不好意思的飛走了。

鐘聲噹～噹～噹～的響起，長頸鹿老師要大家上台自我介紹。

輪到我上台時，我好害怕，站了三秒鐘，不知如何是好。這時台下冒出一些聲音：
「她不會說話嗎？」
我聽了就開始大哭。

這時長頸鹿老師走過來，拍拍我的肩膀，並請台下同學拍手鼓勵我。

老師還幫忙我做自我介紹，讓班上的同學認識我。

上_{ㄕㄤ}學_{ㄒㄩㄝ}後_{ㄏㄡ}，我_{ㄨㄛ}幾_{ㄐㄧ}乎_{ㄏㄨ}天_{ㄊㄧㄢ}天_{ㄊㄧㄢ}都_{ㄉㄡ}會_{ㄏㄨㄟ}哭_{ㄎㄨ}，
因_{ㄧㄣ}為_{ㄨㄟ}別_{ㄅㄧㄝ}人_{ㄖㄣ}都_{ㄉㄡ}不_{ㄅㄨ}知_ㄓ道_{ㄉㄠ}我_{ㄨㄛ}想_{ㄒㄧㄤ}做_{ㄗㄨㄛ}什_{ㄕㄣ}麼_{ㄇㄜ}，
常_{ㄔㄤ}要_{ㄧㄠ}我_{ㄨㄛ}做_{ㄗㄨㄛ}一_ㄧ些_{ㄒㄧㄝ}我_{ㄨㄛ}不_{ㄅㄨ}想_{ㄒㄧㄤ}做_{ㄗㄨㄛ}的_{ㄉㄜ}事_ㄕ。

因ㄧㄣ為ㄨㄟ我ㄨㄛ以ㄧ前ㄑㄧㄢ都ㄉㄡ是ㄕ用ㄩㄥ哭ㄎㄨ來ㄌㄞ表ㄅㄧㄠ達ㄉㄚ，想ㄒㄧㄤ吃ㄔ什ㄕㄣ麼ㄇㄛ，想ㄒㄧㄤ要ㄧㄠ什ㄕㄣ麼ㄇㄛ，只ㄓ要ㄧㄠ我ㄨㄛ一ㄧ哭ㄎㄨ，大ㄉㄚ家ㄐㄧㄚ都ㄉㄡ會ㄏㄨㄟ配ㄆㄟ合ㄏㄜ我ㄨㄛ。

有一天上課時，長頸鹿老師為我設計了一些圖卡，圖卡上面有「上廁所」、「喝水」、「肚子餓」、「不舒服」等圖片，並教我如何去指認圖片來進行溝通。

好棒喔！有了這些圖卡，我就可以用上面的圖片來讓大家知道我想做什麼了。

隔天上課時，長頸鹿老師問大家，如果不會說話，還可以用哪些方法讓別人知道自己想表達什麼呢？

小猴子同學說：「可以用比手畫腳的方式。」

想吃飯

山_{ㄕㄢ}羊_{ㄧㄤ}同_{ㄊㄨㄥ}學_{ㄒㄩㄝ}說_{ㄕㄨㄛ}：「可_{ㄎㄜ}以_ㄧ用_{ㄩㄥ}寫_{ㄒㄧㄝ}的_{ㄉㄜ}。」

白ㄅㄞˊ兔ㄊㄨˋ同ㄊㄨㄥˊ學ㄒㄩㄝˊ說ㄕㄨㄛ：「可ㄎㄜˇ以ㄧˇ用ㄩㄥˋ畫ㄏㄨㄚˋ
的ㄉㄜ呀ㄚ！」

大家都想出好多方法來和我溝通。

現在我知道了，「哭」並不是一種很好的表達方式，也不會是唯一的溝通方法。

大家的了解、包容與接納，讓我可以天天快樂的去上學。我喜歡上學！

給教師及家長的話

透過《美人魚上學趣》這本書，希望能讓孩子在進入一個新環境時，懂得如何與其他人相處，並知道如何幫助有需要的人；也可以從故事中發現「哭」並不是很好的表達及溝通方式，鼓勵孩子試著用不同的方式來表達及解決其所面臨的問題。

在這個故事裡，我們看到美人魚因為無法用聲音來表達，一直都用哭鬧的方式來進行溝通，直到長頸鹿老師提供了協助及教導，美人魚才學會用不同方式——字卡、圖卡等來表達；另外，更重要的是有了同儕的包容與接納，才讓美人魚可以快樂的學習。

在和孩子一起讀完這本繪本後，還可參考筆者所設計的《美人魚上學趣：思做達手冊》。透過手冊，教師及家長能夠了解如何幫助孩子更快且更容易去適應新的環境，讓孩子擁有一個快樂的學習起點。

註：《美人魚上學趣：思做達手冊》可單獨添購，每本定價新台幣 100 元，意者請
　　洽本公司。

Little Mermaid Goes to School

Written by Ying-Ru Meng & Hui-Chu Chen
Illustrated by Chiung-Yau Jang
Translated by Arik Wu

Although I no longer have my voice, now I am able to start my life all over again on the land. It is a brand-new start...

Today, I am going to school. I feel a little excited and scared. I have never left home for school before.

Suddenly, a birdie flies over and stays on a tree. Then he says to me, "Little Mermaid, Little Mermaid, you do not talk, nor do you sing, why are you going to school?"

Upon hearing that, I pull out my flute and play "Twinkle, Twinkle, Little Star" for response.

The birdie looks shamefaced, and then flies away.

Bong! Bong! Bong!

As the school bell tolls, Teacher Giraffe has us go on stage and introduce ourselves.

When it is my turn, I feel so scared. I stand there for three seconds, having no idea what I am supposed to do.

Some classmates of mine ask, "Can't you talk?"

And I start crying out loud.

Teacher Giraffe quickly comes forward to give me a pat on the shoulder and asks the other classmates to give me a round of applause.

Teacher Giraffe introduces me to the other classmates.

On school days, no one seems to understand me. They always ask me to do things I dislike, so I cry almost every day.

When I was younger, I used to communicate with other people through crying. People would do whatever I said as soon as I started crying.

One day, Teacher Giraffe shows me a set of picture cards he designed for me. On these cards, there are pictures of going to toilet room, drinking water, feeling hungry, and not feeling well. He says I can use these picture cards to communicate.

I cannot be happier! With these cards, now I can tell everybody precisely what I want to do!

The next day, Teacher Giraffe raises a question for the class: If a person was unable to talk, what could he or she do to communicate with others?

"Gestures!" Monkey says.

"Writing!" Goat says.

"Drawing!" Rabbit says.

They come up with so many ideas to communicate with me.

Now I understand "crying" will not make things any better, and there are many other ways to communicate! I feel loved, understood, and accepted. I love going to school!